A UNIVERSITY AT PRAYER

A
UNIVERSITY AT PRAYER

BY

ALFRED C. PAYNE

VIRGINIA TECH FOUNDATION

BLACKSBURG, VIRGINIA

1987

Frontispiece by Joni Pienkowski

LIBRARY OF CONGRESS CATALOGING IN PUBLICATION DATA

Payne, Alfred C., 1916-
    A university at prayer.

    Bibliography: p.
    1. universities and colleges—Prayers.
2. Virginia Polytechnic Institute and State
University—Religion.   I. Title.
BV283.C7P39 1987   242′.834   86-14613

ISBN: 0-9617635-0-7

Contents

CONTENTS

A PERSONAL NOTE

MANY people long have encouraged the publication of some of the prayers that I have been privileged to make over many years at Virginia Tech. I regret that I did not attempt the task, although I was truly grateful. Recently Warren Strother and others pulled together a representative selection of the prayers and prepared them for publication. The results are apparent in this volume. I am deeply appreciative. Several members of the Board of the Virginia Tech Foundation personally have contributed very generously to help make this book possible. I am especially grateful to them, as well as to the Foundation itself.

Public prayers in a non-ecclesiastical setting are always difficult, especially in the pluralistic community that is a state university. An inevitable tension exists between fidelity to one's own religious heritage and an essential sensitivity to the feelings of others. If these prayers have a common characteristic, it is their focus upon a specific occasion. So much so that Dr. Warren Brandt, then executive vice president, often chided me for "upstaging the speaker." And Professor John Barringer similarly suggested that I was "instructing the Deity." That certainly was not my intention; rather the prayers were a natural expression of hopes and concerns for a growing university.

Others have noted the recurring use of "O Thou" at the beginning of these invocations. This has little to do with a preference for old English, or the influence of Martin Buber's classic. It rather reflects my discomfort with more informal ways of addressing God. One approaches the Almighty in prayer with confidence and trust, but also with fear and trembling.

ALFRED C. PAYNE

Blacksburg, Virginia
May 1, 1986

AN APPRECIATION

THE Virginia Tech Foundation is indebted to many people for their help in the publication of these selections from the prayers of the Reverend Alfred C. Payne. Virginia Tech President William E. Lavery for some years has attempted to encourage the collection and publication of a representative selection of Mr. Payne's prayers. So, too, did Dr. Lavery's predecessor, Dr. T. Marshall Hahn, Jr. Both made personal contributions toward the cost of publishing this book, in addition to other major support for the University. Mr. Clifford A. Cutchins III, Mr. G. Frank Clement, and Mr. J. S. Hill are other members of the Foundation Board who also made generous personal contributions for this purpose. Mr. C. Eugene Rowe, former chairman and long-time member of the Foundation Board, similarly made a generous contribution.

Mr. Charles M. Forbes, the University's vice president for development and university relations (also vice president of the Foundation), and Dr. Raymond D. Smoot, Jr., associate vice president and treasurer (also secretary-treasurer of the Foundation), have been quite supportive. Mr. Lon K. Savage, executive assistant to the president, Ms. Ann Heidbreder Eastman, staff book publishing officer for the University, and Mr. Edward Born, assistant director of the Water Resources Research Center, all have helped guide the project.

The selection and editing largely was the work of Mr. Warren H. Strother, associate director of Institutional Research and Planning Analysis, and Mr. William T. Walker, Jr., director of Educational Communications. Dr. Wilson C. Snipes, professor of English, corrected most of their errors. The foreword was written by Mr. Strother with the assistance of Mr. Roger E. Comley, associate director of the Donaldson Brown Center for Continuing Education. Mr. Strother also wrote the biographical notes on Mr. Payne.

To these and others whose work made possible the publication of this volume, and to Mr. Payne himself, the Foundation is pleased to acknowledge its sincere appreciation.

THE VIRGINIA TECH FOUNDATION

FOREWORD

IN this small volume may be found the text of some of the prayers of
the Reverend Alfred C. Payne, who for more than two decades
helped to personify the religious concerns of Virginia Tech. They are
representative of hundreds which he wrote and used during his work
on the campus, principally from 1958 until his retirement in 1981. In
those years Mr. Payne's invocations and benedictions came to be a
natural part of official university functions, from special convocations
or campus commemorative events to the annual ROTC commissioning exercises and the June commencement. The selections provide
some insight into the mind of their author, for they suggest the exu-
berant enthusiasm for the intellectual and spiritual mysteries of life
and living which so characterize Al Payne. It is easy to see why he is
beloved by students, colleagues, and others in the university community with whom he worked.

The prayers reflect something of the energy and vitality of the University in the 1960s and 1970s, when Virginia Tech matured into a
comprehensive university. Mr. Payne's latter tenure spanned the administration of President (now president emeritus) T. Marshall Hahn,
Jr., and a good part of those of the late Dr. Walter S. Newman (Dr.
Hahn's predecessor) and President William E. Lavery.

Those who know something of the history of the institution and the
development of higher education in Virginia are aware of the trans-
formation of Virginia Tech in those years. The small, largely male,
military oriented, technical college of which Dr. Newman became
president in 1947 had begun to change significantly before he left
office. Under President Hahn it sustained explosive growth, both in
enrollments and the breadth of its educational programs. President
Lavery has presided over the institution's maturity as a comprehensive university, focused on strengthening the quality of undergraduate
teaching as well as graduate studies and research.

The prayers are interesting, too, from another perspective. To invoke divine blessing on any important occasion is a natural, established practice; many people place high value on this simple habit.
The practice of prayer is an outward reflection of the basic ethical

and spiritual precepts which nearly everyone shares. Yet the appropriateness of prayer in public institutions is sometimes controversial. Some people believe that the absence of prayer is necessary to confirm the separation of church and state. Others believe just as strongly that open prayer is essential to the success of our public institutions. Most simply want to please God properly, to observe etiquette, and avoid offending their neighbors unnecessarily. A keen sensitivity, at least, must underlie the thoughts of those who pray at public events.

The minister praying in church has not only opportunity but the responsibility to see that the special precepts of his religion, indeed of his congregation, are thoroughly woven into his messages to God. Those who pray in public before general audiences have a much more delicate task of pleasing one God and many people at the same time. The prayers in this volume attest with eloquence to the success Mr. Payne achieved in the course of his long career at Virginia Tech.

His prayers are characterized more than anything else by their articulate construction and relevancy to the occasion, always balanced with discretion and good taste. When pronounced aloud, Mr. Payne's prayers fall lightly on the ear and heavily on the conscience. Reading them reveals his dedicated work to God's kingdom on earth and his deep belief in the appropriateness of a university at prayer.

Publication of this limited collection has been long delayed. Marshall Hahn some years ago suggested that Mr. Payne publish a collection of his thoughtful prayers; other friends and colleagues, among them President Lavery, have attempted from time to time to encourage the undertaking. Following Mr. Payne's retirement in 1981 the proposed project languished. Several years elapsed before copies of many of his prayers were brought together, and it was agreed that selections should be published. They are arranged in chronological order (with the exception of the benediction which closes the series), so that the reader might sense something of the changing environment in which the prayers were offered. The volume brings with it much of the joy and effervescent faith which Al Payne has in such full measure.

A UNIVERSITY AT PRAYER

O Thou, in Whose Presence We Naturally Stand

O Thou, in whose presence we naturally stand,
In whose light we see things more clearly,
And in whose ultimate purpose things always make sense,

We simply want to say thanks for all that has
Been done for us, sometimes without our cooperation,
And often without our knowledge,

And to ask for your ready help, your infinite wisdom,
And your clear direction,
Without which our efforts can be wasteful,
And our results even meaningless.

AMEN

Invocation, opening meeting of the Alumni Association, October, 1947.

O Thou, Whom We Call Creator

O Thou, whom we call Creator,
We glorify the creative in man
Through whom we also participate in creation.

Thou whom we call Truth,
We express our gratitude for humor,
Laughter, and even satire
Through which we sometimes see Thee more clearly.

Thou whom from the very beginning art the Word,
We pray that the profusion of words alone
Will not obscure Thy message.

Thou who art characterized as Love itself,
We seek to understand its divine meaning
As well as its human expression.

AMEN

Invocation, "Don Juan in Hell," a group reading in the chapel, March, 1961.

O Thou, to Whom We All Turn

O Thou, to whom we all turn
In high moments of celebration and rededication,

We feel it appropriate, before this ceremony,
To express our gratitude
For those whose part in Thy plan
Has made this moment possible:

For the trust and sacrifice of parents and friends,
For the patience of teachers and administrators,
For the loyalty of those whose lives
      are dedicated to our country,
And for the hopes and aspirations of our future leaders.

Grant us, at this hour,
A renewed understanding of
And devotion to
Words like duty, courage, responsibility.

Help us to see patriotism
As more than mere protection
Of a small bit of geography

But as intelligent concern
For the preservation of values
On which our nation was founded and developed.

Hasten the time when all men will act as brothers,
When all nations can live at peace,
When justice will roll down like waters,
And righteousness as a mighty stream.

AMEN

Invocation, ROTC Commissioning, June, 1962.

The commissioning exercises occur each year just before commencement, when graduating seniors receive their Army, Air Force (and in more recent years, Navy) commissions in special ceremonies.

O Thou Who Doth Transcend

O Thou who doth transcend
Both time and space,
Joy and sorrow,
Matter and spirit,
Persons and things,

We are grateful this morning
That in moments of national crisis,
Of world tensions,
Racial violence,
And personal frustrations,

We can still turn our thoughts
To values beyond the immediate,
Experience the deeper dimensions of creation,
Communicate the heights of human experience,
And get a brief glimpse into man's true nature.

All of which, we trust,
Is part of Thy purpose for us.

AMEN

Invocation, Mark Van Doren Convocation, October, 1962.

The convocation with the renowned critic, poet, and biographer occurred during the Cuban missile crisis, when the Soviets were challenged for placing missiles in Cuba.

Eternal Spirit, May This, Our Spoken Word

Eternal Spirit, may this, our spoken word,
Reveal our true feelings, and our honest hopes.

Deliver us, we pray,

From selfish pride in past accomplishments
Into fresh enthusiasm for new opportunities;

From the lazy assumption that the world owes us a living
Into responsible recognition that society is what we make it;

From irresponsible criticism of parents, teachers, and institutions
Into healthy respect for all those who helped us to be here today;

From selfish attitudes of promoting ourselves
Into intelligent concern for the welfare of all;

From doing a lot of things shabbily
Into the joy of doing a few things well;

From an immature satisfaction with a narrow religious life
Into a wholesome experience of spiritual growth;

From the false idols of comfort, popularity, and power,
Into faith that there is a reliable truth which can be known,

And that this truth can keep us free.

AMEN

Invocation, Commencement, June, 1964.

The commencement exercises then were held in the coliseum, later named Cassell Coliseum. In later years, as the number of people attending the commencement programs increased so rapidly, the annual ceremony was moved to Lane Stadium.

When I Consider Thy Heavens

When I consider Thy heavens, the work of Thy fingers,
The moon and the stars which Thou has ordained,
What is Man, that Thou are mindful of him?

O Thou who art God of the psalmists and shepherds,
Of poets and astronauts,
Open our minds this morning
To new and unlimited horizons
Of time and space.

Give us that mixture of confidence and humility,
Of understanding and awe,
That we might go from here
Grateful for a vision of a new heaven
But also with an intelligent concern
For building a new earth.

AMEN

Invocation for a convocation with Fred Hoyle, the British mathematician and astronomer, December, 1964.

For the Courage to Stimulate Creative Thinking

For the courage to stimulate creative thinking,
Even unthinkable thoughts,
In a time of fear and conformity;

For the imagination and concern
That link peoples of the world
With a chain of scholarship,
Instead of slavery;

For recognition that study and research
Are not bound by the earlier rules
Of nation and geography;

For the example of relating love of the University
With an intelligent concern for the universe;

For the privilege this morning
Of witnessing to these values,
And meeting one who has wrapped them all
In one personality:

We respectully express our gratitude
And hopefully trust
That many of us will catch the vision
In Thy holy name.

AMEN

Invocation for a convocation with J. William Fulbright, April, 1965. He then was the U.S. Senator from Arkansas, in which office he served for 30 years. Senator Fulbright initiated the international exchange program for scholars which bears his name.

O Thou Who Has Created Us All

O Thou, who has created us all,
And who, as Nature's God, has endowed us
With such inalienable rights
As life, liberty, and the pursuit of happiness,

We here today reaffirm those truths,
Proclaimed self-evident by this nation's founders:
The priority of man above the State,
Equality under the law,
And government by consent of the governed.

And we renew our dedication to freedom
And independence,
Both at home and abroad.

In the spirit of our fathers
We gratefully salute these, Thy sons,
Who, with firm reliance on the protection
Of Thy Divine Providence,

And with a decent respect
For the opinions of mankind,

Are this day, and in our presence,

Pledging their lives,
Their fortunes,
And their sacred honor.

AMEN

Invocation, ROTC Commissioning Exercises, June, 1965.

O God of the Spacious Skies

O God of the spacious skies,
Of whom we sing,
And to whom we pray,

Whose grace has been so generously shed
On this nation and its people,

And whose limitless horizons beckon
To our most adventurous spirits,

Do crown the good and great achievements of these, our sons,
With eventual brotherhood of all Thy peoples.

And as we are met here to honor one
Who already has honored us,

Help us to see that in recognizing
    Responsibility,
    Perseverance,
    And intelligent concern
      for the lives of others,
We are also doing honor to Thee.

AMEN

Invocation, testimonial program honoring Christopher C. Kraft '45, then director of the National Aeronautics and Space Administration's Manned Spacecraft Center at Houston, Texas, November, 1965.

The nation was excited about Projects Mercury and Gemini, the first major steps toward fulfilling President John Kennedy's pledge to put a man on the moon in the decade of the 1960s.

O Thou Who Art Creator of Us All

O Thou who art Creator of us all
And for whom all creatures have meaning and value,

We open this convocation with gratitude
   for all creative spirits,
For those whose skill with words and
   sensitivity to ideas
Have opened wider doors to understanding.

We who have become preoccupied with communication
Confess our failure at times to listen.
We who are concerned with easy answers
Confess our tendency to postpone basic questions.
We who are proud of machines that almost think
Confess our reluctance to think for ourselves.

Inspire us, we pray, with Thy Presence at this hour;
Cleanse our hearts;
Quicken our minds;
And relax our bodies.

Give us a glimpse of the real beyond the phony
And of the ultimate truth beneath the facts.

Breathe upon the flickering spark of our own creative talents
And send us back to our jobs enriched.

This we pray in the name of Him
Who from the very beginning
Was the Word.

AMEN

Invocation for a convocation with Poet John Ciardi, October, 1965.

O Thou, Through Whom We Find Gratitude

O Thou, through whom we find gratitude
To honor five great educators,

We would discern anew
The highest goals and purpose of education itself.

O Thou, to whom we also dedicate these new buildings,
Help us rededicate ourselves as well.

O Thou, who has assured us all of immortality,
We pray that the names of men like these
Will continue to honor the name
   of a growing university
Whose life and work is meaningless
Apart from thine Own Name,

In which we pray.

AMEN

Invocation, dedication of five new residence halls, May 16, 1966. The halls were named, respectively, for C. P. "Sally" Miles, T. S. A. Johnson, Walter S. Newman, Charles E. Vawter, and Paul B. Barringer.

With Gratitude and Inspiration, God

With gratitude and inspiration, God,
We meet on this historic spot
To show respect to genius
And pay tribute to generosity.

We are grateful for institutions
As lengthened shadows of great men,
For the cooperative spirit
Between family and government,
    industry and education,
And for contributions of agriculture
    to the culture of us all.

We are inspired by truths remembered here:
That by sowing hard work and big ideas
We reap less toil,
That when we plant concern for human welfare
We harvest genius and generosity.

And with this gratitude and inspiration, God,
We somehow sense thine own clear plan:

The proper relation between men and machines,
A proper kinship between soil and soul,
All of which are in Thy constant care.

AMEN

Invocation, dedication of Cyrus McCormick Farm as a national historic landmark,
June, 1966.

McCormick Farm, at Steele's Tavern, was the ancestral home of the McCormicks,
where Cyrus McCormick developed the reaper in 1831. The Shenandoah Valley
farm had been a gift to Virginia Tech from the McCormick family for use as an
agricultural experiment station. The old McCormick mill and its mill and shop
where the grain reaper was perfected is now a historic shrine.

When We Turn Our Thoughts to Thee, O God

When we turn our Thoughts to Thee, O God,

We think more of others than of ourselves,
More of greatness than of expediency,
More of things that must be done
Than of things we'd like to do.

And with Thy Spirit guiding us
We can

Be prepared for conflict
And still work hard for peace,
Strengthen ourselves in discipline
And still have personal freedom,
Be loyal to a cause worth dying for
And still value life itself,
Accept our own responsibility
And still confess that we depend on Thee.

AMEN

ROTC Commissioning Exercises, June, 1966.

O Thou Before Whom We All Stand, Quietly and Uncovered

O Thou before whom we all stand, quietly and uncovered,

Let our standing show true reverence,
 our silence, teachability,
 and our bowed heads, an honest humility.

May these our opening words of prayer
 and our initial gesture of respect
 set the tone for this significant occasion.

And as this moment of gratitude precedes this hour of celebration,
 may the hour itself
 provide the finishing touch
 to years of work

And a real commencement
 to heroic days ahead.

AMEN

Invocation, Commencement, June, 1966.

We Are Grateful Tonight, God, for a Lot of Things

We are grateful tonight, God, for a lot of things:

For an institution that still recognizes the place
    of prayer at significant occasions,
For education that transcends the limits
    of time and space,
For the continuing influence of students far beyond
    the campus,
And for the spirit of Alma Mater
    that originally influenced them,
For fond memories and great expectations,
    and for much, much more.

Help us, O God, to deserve these gifts
    and to build upon them.
Unite us all with a vision of greatness,
    and keep before us the goal of our highest calling,

In Jesus, who is called the Christ.

AMEN

Invocation, Chapter Officers' Campus Forum, The Alumni Association, October, 1967.

Accept Our Thanks, O God

Accept our thanks, O God,

For the ability to laugh,
    especially at ourselves,

For a healthy sense of humor
    in times of trouble,

And for the universal smile
    in a world of pain.

Help us all to take a joke
    as well as tell one;

To see the truth behind a twinkle
    and hidden meaning behind a tear.

Save us, we pray,
    from taking ourselves too seriously,

Thus missing the point
    behind it all.

AMEN

Invocation for a convocation with Bennett Cerf, the humorist and publisher, November 16, 1967.

O Thou, Who Created Heaven and Earth

O Thou, who created heaven and earth,
Who made man in Thine own image,
And who desires for all an abundant life,
We are grateful for the opportunity to think
    Thy Thoughts after Thee.
Help us to see Thee not as a stop-gap for our
    present limited knowledge
But rather as one whose greatness is even more
    revealed as our awareness of Thy laws increase.

May we continue to build upon the past
    but not be bound by it.
Keep our eyes open to new forms as well as new truths
    in a time of accelerated change,
And give us the vision and stamina to use machines
    as our servants and not let them become our masters.

We pray particularly
That we may grow in understanding of ourselves
As we continue to unlock the mysteries of nature,

That we may never lose sight of the human dimension
    in our growing control of time and space,
That we can retain an appreciation of spirit
    as well as matter and understand the implications
Of theology as well as technology.

Renew in us a respect for the proven old, as well
    as the untried new.
May we not lose our sense of purpose in our preoccupation
    with method,
And may we be concerned with ways of life rather than
    means of death.

This we address to Thee whom we call God,
Whose Thoughts are still beyond our own,

To whom miracles can be routine,
And in whose name all things are made new.

AMEN

Invocation, convocation with Dr. Simon Ramo, then vice chairman of TRW, Inc., March 8, 1968.

The corporation previously had given Virginia Tech a major industrial testing facility near Smith Mountain Lake in Franklin County.

O Thou, to Whom We Naturally Turn

O Thou, to whom we naturally turn
    in moments like this,
Whose spirit transcends life and death,
And in Whom we find meaning
    even in periods of conflict,
We are here in a spirit
Of holy days, not just holidays.

In the spirit of Veterans' Day
We want to show our awareness
    of what a devoted few have done
    for the grateful many.

In the spirit of Thanksgiving
We want to express our gratitude
    for the lives of these fine men,
For their contribution
    to this University and this nation,
For their example at a time
    when old values are being questioned,
And for their witness that some of these values
Are still worth giving our lives for.

In the spirit of Christmas, too,
    a time of giving and receiving,
We are reminded of Him who once lived
    as one of us,
Whose life was one of joy in spite of suffering,
Courage, as well as love,
    and sacrifice without complaint.
Let us, we pray, not forget this day,
And in the name of Him whose spirit still lives,

> Let us engrave upon our lives
> > the memory of those whose names
> > are engraved on the stones above.

AMEN

Special retreat ceremony, November 22, 1968.

The military ceremony honored Virginia Tech alumni who gave their lives for their country. Their names earlier had been engraved on the tall pylons atop the War Memorial.

O Thou Who First Used a Simple Meal

O Thou who first used a simple meal
To dramatize the ideal relationship between people,
And to demonstrate the concern You have for all of us,
We express our gratitude this morning for Dietrick Hall,
For the man for whom it is named,
For the purpose for which it stands,
And for the University it will serve.

AMEN

Invocation, dedication of Dietrick Dining Hall, May 11, 1970.

The new dining hall was named in honor of L. B. "Deet" Dietrick, dean emeritus of the College of Agriculture and Life Sciences.

O Thou, Without Whom We Would Not Even Be

O Thou, without whom we would not even be,
    much less be here,
And without whom this food would not be a possibility,
    much less a reality,
We begin this significant occasion
    in an attitude of prayer.
We are grateful for the spirit of joy
    in a day of sadness,
For the show of appreciation
    in a time of ingratitude,
And for the demonstration of unity
    in a world of confrontation.
Bless, we pray, this food and this occasion,
And make us worthy of both.

AMEN

Invocation, Senior Honors Banquet, May 5, 1971.

The senior honors banquet, held each spring for many years, honored outstanding seniors.

O Thou, Who Created Trees of the Forest

O Thou, who created trees of the forest,
    With all other forms of life,
    And placed them in man's keeping,
Help us to be responsible participants
    In Thy creation:
In recreation of persons,
    And recreation of natural resources.

O Thou, who art the source of life itself,
Help us to protect thine unlimited resources:
    To use them, not abuse them;
    Multiply them, not destroy them.

O Thou, who has brought us here to dedicate this building,
    Help us to dedicate ourselves as well
    To rebuilding Thy world—and ours.

AMEN

Invocation, dedication of Julian Cheatham Hall, May 5, 1972.

The building name honors Mr. Julian N. Cheatham '33, of Portland, Oregon, a retired Georgia-Pacific Corporation executive, who helped make possible construction of the facility.

Our Invocation, Lord, Is Both Confession and Petition

Our invocation, Lord, is both confession and petition,
And reveals much more than we can say:
That there are profound questions for which we have no
    simple answer
And complex forces which we cannot control.

But that there are also forces which have our interest at the
    very heart of things
And divine wisdom available which transcends our human
    limitations.

We represent many disciplines, but one truth;
Many interests, but one concern;
Many publics, but one Commonwealth;
Many perspectives, but one God.

Let us, with Thy help, be truly inspired by the significance of
    this conference.
May we not be too awed by our second century, nor too encumbered
    by the first.

Help us to see things as they really are, but also as they ought to be.
Keep our eyes on the stars and our feet on the ground.

Your prophets have said that without vision the people perish.
So let us share our noblest dreams;
Then help us, we pray, to turn them into reality,
Remembering, as we work together, that we are searching for
    the City,

Whose builder and maker is God.

AMEN

Invocation, Conference on Higher Education, Second Century Emphasis Week, October, 1972. The conference was part of the year-long observance of the centennial of the University's founding.

O Thou, Whom We Worship in Different Ways

O Thou, whom we worship in different ways,
We are united this morning by gratitude for the past,
High hopes for the future,
And a loyalty to Alma Mater, whose sons and daughters
Have brought distinction to our name.

Help us, as we face the years ahead,
To build upon the best of our heritage,
To understand the difference between bigness and greatness,
And to be known for our well-being, as well as our being well known.

If we are inclined to rest upon our laurels,
Challenge us to greater things.
When our purposes become blurred, sharpen them;
When our values become confused, help us to clarify them;
And where we happen to be wrong, help us to see the right.

When our principles are compromised.
Strengthen them with Thy truth,
And help us to strive, all the time,
To translate the words of our motto, "That I may Serve,"
Into responsible action.

AMEN

Invocation, Founders Day, April 19, 1973.

The University began the annual commemoration of its founding as part of the centennial observance in 1972, with March 19, 1872, as its official birthday. The annual observance rarely is on March 19, however, because of the need to accommodate the current academic calendar.

Let Us First Give Thanks

Let us first give thanks,
For the seniors here tonight
Who have made us proud of our vocation.
We give Thee thanks, O God,
For minds that keep us humble and spirits which keep us young;
For unselfish service which gives the word "honor" real meaning;
For leaders who pull instead of push
And for education which never ends.

We give Thee thanks
For common causes that transcend age and point of view,
And for common sense which helps us work together.
For light hearts, willing hands, and healthy appetites,
And most of all for Thy Divine love
Which made it all possible,
We give Thee our sincere thanks.

AMEN

Invocation, Senior Honors Banquet, May, 1973.

O Thou, Who Comes to Us in Many Ways

O Thou, who comes to us in many ways,
In art as beauty, in science as truth,
We acknowledge Thee in our moment of joy and celebration.

O Thou, whom we can see in nature as law,
In history as justice, and in humanity as love,
We confess our failure to seek Thy purpose
Or to follow Thy will.

O Thou, who has shown Thyself through the years
In scripture, tradition, and experience,
We express our gratitude for
The integrity of language,
The divinity of ideas,
And the sacredness of relationships.

Thou, in whom the art of living and the science of life
Somehow become one with each other,
We ask for the wisdom to recognize
All symbols of Thy creation,
All media of Thy revelation,
And all instruments of Thy salvation.

AMEN

Invocation, College of Arts and Sciences Commencement Exercises, June 9, 1973.

O Thou Who Art Beyond Definition

O Thou who art beyond definition,
Whose greatness we cannot comprehend,
And whose goodness we do not always deserve,
Help us to understand that commencement means "beginning"
And not an end to aspirations,
And that the more we learn the more we realize we do not know.

In this time of moral confusion,
When loyalties are unclear and even suspect,
Push us to the highest loyalty we can affirm:
Beyond academic disciplines or religious denominations,
Beyond institution or party, nation or race,
To the most ultimate of values,
The holiest of holies, the everlasting God.

Forgive us, not so much for missing the target
But for taking low aim.
Give us the long view,
A vision that's unlimited,
And keep our eyes on the farthest horizon,
The most distant star.

Stretch our minds to their infinite possibilities,
And let us remain unsatisfied with a partial revelation
Until we get a glimpse of truth itself.

AMEN

Invocation, Commencement, June, 1973.

O Lord Who Has Been Our Real Dwelling Place

O Lord who has been our real dwelling place
In all generations,

Help us this morning
To see 'way beyond the easy words
And the visual impressions
Of the occasion;

To realize
That in our dedication of this building
We are aware of the dedication
To the University of the one
For whom it is named;

That just as the building itself
Is so clearly recognized across the campus,
The University still recognizes those persons
Who stand out in their loyalty to its mission;

That a structure built for service
To thousands of students in future years
Bears the name of one who served their
Mothers and fathers in years past,
And that one designed so carefully
For meaningful living in the University
Will continue to nourish the spirit of those
Who have given it much of their lives.

AMEN

Invocation, Dedication of Slusher Hall, May 3, 1974.

The residence hall for women was named in honor of Mrs. Clarice Slusher Prichard, who had served as registrar during 1937-1963.

O Thou Who Art the Source of Life and Love

O Thou, who art the source of life and love
And the ultimate source of energy itself
We who profess that "the earth is the Lord's"
Have fallen short of our obligations as trustees.

We are grateful today for individuals
And for institutions,
Who show intelligent concern
For Thy world and its people.

Give us, we pray,
The insight to understand Thy secrets.
The ability to share this with others,
And the will to persevere,
Even in times of crisis.

Finally, save us from both naivete and short-sightedness,
And hasten the day when our theories become practical
And the ideal becomes real.

AMEN

Invocation, Colloquy on Energy Resources, College of Agriculture and Life Sciences, January 23, 1975.

Our Hearts, O Lord, Are Filled with Gratitude
for Many Things

Our hearts, O Lord, are filled with gratitude for many things:

For lives that are being dedicated to the protection of our homes and
    loved ones,
For homes that have continued to nourish a love of country
    and its values,
And for a country that today is not at war with other nations.

Our hearts are heavy, though,
That this same nation now seems to be at war with itself:
That the honor of some of its institutions is being tarnished,
That some elected leaders have betrayed their trust,
And that so many citizens are more concerned with themselves
Than with problems of our country.
Help us, we pray, to reaffirm those values which have made this
    nation great
And to renew our appreciation for traditions that seek to
    preserve them.

Give us, we pray, the wisdom to understand that precarious balance
Between freedom and discipline.
Save us from confusing freedom with individual selfishness
And from mistaking discipline for tyranny.
Help us, somehow, to see that disciplined individuals are essential
To a nation's freedom,
Whereas freedom for the self alone can lead to an undisciplined
    nation.

We ask this, O God, because Thou are our Ultimate Authority.
And we pray in the name of Him in whose service we find perfect
    freedom.

AMEN

Invocation, ROTC Commissioning Exercises, June, 1976.

We Need Not Invoke Thy Presence, God

We need not invoke Thy presence, God,
For we know You are already here.

Whenever we hungered after truth and beauty, You were there.
And whenever we put the welfare of others ahead of ourselves,
It was You who inspired us.

Without You we would not have felt concern over injustice
Or enjoyed new opportunities after a bad start.
Without You we could not have worked for harmony between
    groups.
Or reconciliation between people.
You were always there when we heard a forgiving word, or an
    encouraging one,
Or when our silent prayers were answered,
    even when the answer was "No."

We have felt Thy spirit in the inspiration of books and teachers
And in the sudden awareness that we were not alone in time of
    trouble.
You have been present, Lord, in the sacrifices our loved ones made,
So that we could arrive at this moment of celebration
In a guilty conscience as well as in our satisfaction in a job well done.

You were always there when we had a clear vision of what is right,
In our disdain for hypocrisy and laziness,
In our willingness to get involved, rather than criticize,
In the quiet feeling of confidence that things would somehow
    work out,
In the discovery of new truth, or the creation of a new design,
And in the awareness of a greater unity of which we are a part.

In countless ways, O Lord, some of which we cannot appreciate
   until years later,
You have been with us all and will continue to bless us.

God, make us truly grateful, for Thy sake and ours.

AMEN

Invocation, Commencement, June, 1976.

Help Us, O God, To See the True Meaning
Behind Celebration

Help us, O God, to see the true meaning behind celebration
    and ceremony,
To see profound truths beyond symbol and ritual,
And to put real flesh on the words we have heard and spoken
As we celebrate our nation's Bicentennial.

Let each of us here today affirm our own declaration of
    independence
From shallow thinking and selfish attitudes.
And let the memory of this occasion
Help us to follow those principles
So that in turn we may lead others.

AMEN

Benediction, Bicentennial Observance, July 4, 1976.

O Thou, Who Dared Reveal Thyself
(A Christmas Prayer)

O Thou, who dared reveal Thyself
By coming down as one of us,
And who can best be understood
Through symbols seen this time of year,

Give us, we pray, the faith and skill
To grasp the truth of candlelight
And rethink goals with every star;
Seek harmony through every song
And feel more joy with every chime;
To nurture faith at home and hearth,
Discover hope through winter greens,
And sense great love in little gifts.

May we still find eternal truths
Behind the story, told anew:
How tidings came to simple folk
While they were on their jobs;
How wise men came from other lands,
With skin of different hue;
And of the birth in darkest night
Which opened up a great new day.

Let this, a prayer for holidays,
Prepare us for the Holy Day
And for another priceless gift:
A brand new year of life,
A grand new chance for all,
And time to work for peace.

AMEN

Invocation, Extension staff luncheon, December 15, 1976. The prayer was entitled
"A Prayer for Holidays" in Mr. Payne's collection.

O Thou, Whom We Cannot See, nor Measure, nor Understand

O Thou, whom we cannot see, nor measure, nor understand,
   whom we too frequently disobey, but to whom we still turn
   freely in moments of memory and hope,

We are grateful to be a part of an institution that still believes
   in prayer.

We are grateful, too, for an institution that remembers,
   that recognizes, that appreciates.

We are here to remember the past, to celebrate the present, and
   to anticipate the future.

Be with us now as we honor the contributions of others, and help us
   to gain new inspiration as we prepare for the challenges ahead.

Let us learn from the past without worshipping it and prepare
   for the future without fear.

Keep before us the significant missions of this University, teaching,
   research, and extension, so that we shall never forget the value
   of persons, the power of truth, and the joys of service.

AMEN

Invocation, Founders Day Exercises, March, 1977.

Our Hearts, O God, Are Glad for Many Reasons

Our hearts, O God, are glad for many reasons,
And our thoughts are filled with gratitude for many things:

For our feelings of accomplishment,
Our sense of completion,
And our spirit of anticipation.

Help us, we pray, to live this moment to the fullest,

Remembering still
All those who have come before,
Upon whose shoulders we are able to stand tonight,

Plus all those present—and absent—who made this event possible,
And those who will come later on,
Whose lives will be different
Because of what we may have done.

AMEN

Invocation, Senior Honors Banquet, May, 1977.

O Thou, Who Transcends Time and Space

O Thou, who transcends time and space, individuals and institutions,

Regardless of our background, or how we might address You,
    we are all alike at this moment in our sense of gratitude.

But we also have a mixture of feelings, of satisfaction and
    disappointment, of pride and apprehension.
But that's what life is all about.

We have learned much from each other which we will take with us,
    but learning will still go on.
For that's the way things are.

Keep us aware that some solutions are not final and that happiness
    is not always easy.
For that's the way it is.

Help us, we pray, to be grateful that things are not always simple,
    nor the direction always clear, and even though the world
    sometimes looks too big, or too uncertain,
Therein lies the challenge.

O Thou, who can bring reason out of ambiguity and order out of
    confusion, we are glad You have been with us all along,
    and we sense Thy spirit is with us now.
For That's what gives meaning to it all.

AMEN

Invocation, Commencement, May, 1977.

O Thou, Who Art the God of Us All

O Thou, who art the God of us all,
Who transcends personal convictions and institutional loyalties,
To whom youth and age, here and there, then and now,
Are all one,

We are grateful for the balanced values dramatized here,
For both wisdom and creativity, for both tradition and change.

We are particularly glad for the feeling of good will
Between those with different perspectives and responsibilities,
For the joyful experience of building bridges across the
    generation gap,
For young ideas that keep a university relevant,
And for older structures which make them work.

We are grateful, too, for both pleasant memories and exciting hopes.
Let us look backward, not with sadness but with gratitude,
And look forward, not with fear but expectation.

Help us to understand the need we all have for each other
And that this need will continue and grow.
And as we demonstrate tonight the "Uni" in University
And concentrate its many lessons in "one verse,"
Let us see that it is all part of one tremendous idea, One God,
In whose master plan it all fits
And to whom it is beautiful, harmonious, and right.

AMEN

Invocation, Senior Honors Banquet, May 2, 1979.

O Thou, Who Art the Alpha and Omega

O Thou, who art the Alpha and Omega,
The first and the last, the beginning and the end,
Help us to see that Commencement is not just the end of an
    experience
But the "commencing" of another.

Thou to whom "a Thousand years in Thy sight
Are but as yesterday, when it is past,"
Let us see that true education is always continuous
And that learning never ends.

Thou who art both the Source and the Goal of our aspirations,
Help us to fit this brief exciting moment
Into the span of a lifetime,
And even into eternity itself.

Thou whose love for us transcends both time and space,
Help us to convert our memories of the past into hopes for the future.
And though we now may "see through a glass darkly,"
Let us someday see truth face to face.

Help us, we pray,
To see that our years here were not just preparation for living
But a piece of life itself,
To place our lives now into that unique position which is waiting
    for us
And to feel not like a cog in a great machine
But rather as a free person with a vital role in Thy divine plan.

AMEN

Invocation, Commencement, June 9, 1979.

O Thou, Who Offers Solace in Time of Sadness

O Thou, who offers solace in time of sadness,
And who can even bring joy in the midst of sorrow,
We gather tonight in both gratitude and celebration,
Grateful for the life of one of us who was privileged to go on ahead,
Yet celebrating his contribution, too, to our common cause.

We are proud, O God, of these seniors, and not a little proud of
    ourselves.
Forgive us if we point with pride so much this evening
While others are viewing the world with alarm.
As this, our university family, gathers around Thy table,
Let Thy spirit of love and understanding be our host.

As we move from the world of ideas and experimentation
Into the world of action and responsibility,
When the classroom changes to home and office,
And student life suddenly becomes vocation and citizenship,
Help us to shift easily from the attitude of play
To a time when we must play for keeps.

Give us new solutions to match new problems,
Fresh ideas for worn-out structures,
And constant hope for a time of despair.

Help these senior leaders, we pray,
To retain their freshness in a world gone stale,
To retain their idealism, when it's so easy to be cynical,
And to retain their vigor and strength when so many are weak.

Give them, we pray, continued appreciation for Alma Mater,
And let our own pride grow in their later accomplishments.
Help them to recall, every day of their lives,

That he or she who is greatest is servant of all.
And somehow, let us all manage to give Thee the glory
    and not try to keep it ourselves.

AMEN

Invocation, Senior Honors Banquet, May 7, 1980.

Mr. Payne a few hours earlier had conducted a memorial service for John Taylor
Fearnow III, a 21-year-old senior who had accidentally drowned in the New
River.

O Thou Who Has Planted the Seeds of Loyalty

O Thou who has planted the seeds of loyalty, discipline,
And love of country within our being,
We ask today for a clearer vision of Thy will for this nation
And Thy purpose in our own lives.
Help us to nourish proper idealism without becoming naive
And develop confidence without becoming arrogant.

Give us, we pray,
Pride without conceit,
Strength without bluster,
Dedication without fanaticism,
And respect without fear.
And with this vision of what is right
Give us the will to perform our duty with unselfishness and honor.

AMEN

Invocation, ROTC Commissioning Exercises, June 7, 1980.

O Thou, Who Art the Source of All Our Concern
for Each Other

O Thou, who art the source of all our concern for each other,
Help us to see that what is ours, is not ours alone,
And whatever enhances our own welfare is best when shared.
Enlarge our vision, widen our interests, expand our skills,
    and deepen our concerns.

We pray in the name of Him
In whose service is perfect freedom
And in whose will is our ultimate peace.

AMEN

Invocation, luncheon for Dr. Arturo Tanco, Minister of Agriculture, Republic of the Philippines, May 9, 1980.

O Thou in Whom We Live and Move
and Have Our Being

O Thou in whom we live and move and have our being,
We are glad that we are never far away from You
And from Your loving concern for our welfare.

We acknowledge Thy presence in all that we do
And are grateful tonight, particularly that we can enjoy each other.

O Thou who turned the water into wine
And whom the people were always glad to have around,
We are especially grateful for Thy wonderful gifts
Of food, and music, and conversation.

Bless, we pray, this occasion and all its participants,
And all that symbolizes Thy concern for our welfare.

Let us make a joyful noise
And then go out and serve Thee
With even more gladness.

AMEN

Invocation, Virginia Tech Faculty and Staff Dinner Dance, March 14, 1981.

O Thou Who Art the Father of All People

O Thou who art the Father of all people,
Ruler of all nations,
King of the universe,
We come before you with a mixture
Of gratitude and dedication,
Facing the future with both confidence and uncertainty.

Let us not be so preoccupied with problems and difficulties
That we forget the blessings and advantages
Which already are ours.

Keep before us those qualities which are everlasting,
Like character, loyalty, and courage,
And not just those temporal things
Like wealth, and fame, and power.

Help us to appreciate the true meaning of patriotism
Amid constant challenge of a world that is not free.

Let us always deserve to be pleased with ourselves,
But better yet, let us seek to please Thee.
Give us visions of high goals
And the ability to attain them,
Remembering that in all things,
If we acknowledge Thee,
Thou will direct our paths.

AMEN

Invocation, ROTC Commissioning Exercises, June, 1981.

We Now Must Say "Farewell," O God

We now must say "farewell," O God, to old friends and old places,
  but we look forward to saying "greetings" to new ones.

We leave a bit of ourselves here: ideas, attitudes, and heritage.
But we take much more with us as well: fond memories, valuable
  experience, and significant relationships.

With thankfulness for the help of others and loyalty to our
  Alma Mater, help us to look forward with confidence in ourselves,
  and with continued trust in Thee.

AMEN

Benediction, Commencement, May, 1977.

Biographical Notes

THE REVEREND ALFRED C. PAYNE was ordained at Blacksburg Baptist Church in 1947, while serving an initial assignment at Virginia Tech as associate secretary of the Campus YMCA. He grew up in Cartersville, Georgia, where his father was yardmaster for the Louisville & Nashville Railroad and his mother was (as the younger Payne later characterized her) "a community shoulder on which people could lean." Their son enrolled initially in engineering at Clemson University; he later switched fields and earned a degree in general sciences. He also won a scholarship to Yale Divinity School, where he enrolled in 1938.

Those first years at Yale were difficult, especially because Payne had to earn a living as well as meet a heavy academic schedule. He left the university without his degree to accept appointment as a staff member of the Campus YMCA at Texas A&M University. When World War II began, Payne moved to a regional assignment in Texas for the Office of Civil Defense. A year later he entered the U. S. Army as an infantry lieutenant and soon found himself in combat in Europe.

It is perhaps ironic that the young man who later so personified peace and Christian love achieved such an outstanding military record. Among other things, he won a battlefield promotion to the rank of captain and left the service in 1945 a much-decorated combat veteran. After the war he went back to Yale to complete his theological studies. In 1946, with a newly earned divinity degree, he accepted the YMCA assignment at Virginia Tech and began working with the late Paul Derring.

The Y at Virginia Tech in those days was an extension of the institution. For practical purposes its functions included many of those of a student personnel group, dealing with student activities and concerns. Those were the days when the veterans came back from World War II, overflowing the campus, and civilian students first began to outnumber the Corps of Cadets. Derring, Payne, and other Y staff obviously had their hands full. He would later characterize his initial years at Virginia Tech as "an excellent learning experience."

Payne's work at Virginia Tech was followed by five years as secretary of the Campus YMCA at the University of Pittsburgh, which he found satisfying and productive. In the mid-fifties, however, he accepted a challenging special assignment for the YMCA, attempting to ease the problems of previously all-white Southern universities as they began to admit black students. Payne returned to Virginia Tech as general secretary of the campus YMCA in 1958.

The legendary Paul Derring, the blind Y leader who served Virginia Tech some forty-five years, earlier had left the leadership of the Y to serve as director of campus religious activities. The late Orrin McGill, a one-time Y secretary at Virginia Tech who had served the YMCA in China for many years, filled in for a year prior to Payne's return to the campus. Payne himself was moved from the Y staff to the student personnel staff in 1964 when Paul Derring retired.

For the next seventeen years Al Payne was the personification of Virginia Tech's religious and spiritual concerns. While he represented both the religious community and the state university, he concerned himself very little with the ambiguity of such a position in terms of the separation of church and state. In the latter years of his work at Virginia Tech he was designated "coordinator of religious affairs," which seemed appropriately descriptive.

Shortly after Payne returned to Virginia Tech, the War Memorial was completed; in 1960 it was formally dedicated, a gift to the University by its alumni. Beneath the tall pylons of the War Memorial is Memorial Chapel, a beautiful, quiet place for meditation or worship. In the last few years of his work at the University, Payne maintained an office in a small room off the chapel, perhaps his favorite place on the campus.

Payne is married to the former Miss Virle Crow, of Fairforest, South Carolina. They met as young participants at a religious retreat in the North Carolina mountains and were married during Payne's service at Texas A&M University, just prior to World War II. Mrs. Payne is a graduate of Winthrop College and studied also at the University of Tennessee, Temple University, and Virginia Tech. She is a former member of the faculty of the College of Home Economics (now Human Resources) at Virginia Tech and retired in 1982 from Radford University, where she taught child development and nursery school education. The couple has a son, Thomas E. Payne of Roanoke, and two daughters, Mrs. John M. (Ann) Graham, of Birmingham, Alabama, and Miss Ginny Payne of Tampa, Florida.

Since the Paynes' retirement they have traveled extensively, most recently to China, Mexico, and Canada. They remain, fortunately, very much a part of the university community, immersed in a wide range of civic and university-related activities. Recently OΔK (Omicron Delta Kappa), the honorary leadership society, established the annual Alfred C. Payne service award in Al Payne's honor. The establishment of the new OΔK award, for service to the university community, delighted him. It couldn't have been more timely.

AN EDITION OF

ONE THOUSAND COPIES OF

A UNIVERSITY AT PRAYER

HAS BEEN COMPOSED IN LINOTYPE CALEDONIA

AND PRINTED LETTERPRESS BY THE SHAGBARK PRESS IN

SOUTH PORTLAND, MAINE. THE TEXT PAPER IS

SUPERFINE, AN ACID-FREE SHEET

MADE BY MOHAWK PAPER

MILLS.

————————

DESIGN BY HARRY MILLIKEN